Anxiety

Overcome Relationship Anxiety By Utilizing Rumination Coping Strategies, Implementing Effective Communication Practices, And Discovering The Key To Maintaining Happy Long-term Romances

(A Comprehensive Manual For Embracing An Expansive And Exquisite Existence)

Francesco Corradini

TABLE OF CONTENT

Disorder of Separation Anxiety 1

Teenage Anxiety and the Brain 8

How do we stop thinking bad thoughts? 19

Anxiety's Effects on the Body 37

ASSISTING YOUR AUTISM-SUFFERING CHILD TO LIVE 71

Individual Connections 83

The Effects of Anxiety and Stress 95

Recognising social anxiety, its warning signs, and its risks 123

The Nervous System: An Essential Organ! 138

Disorder of Separation Anxiety

When we are attached to someone or something, being parted from them can make us feel nervous or depressed. However, we may have a separation anxiety disorder if this fear becomes overwhelming or chronic. While it is more frequent in youngsters, adults can also be affected by this disorder. Among the warning signs to watch out for is ● Constantly fretting while contemplating breaking up with someone or something ● experiencing overwhelming anxiety associated with being alone or apart from the attachment figure ●, envisioning dire situations in which you might lose or be separated from the "attachment figure."

● reluctant to sleep in the attachment figure's absence

● Consistently displaying certain physical or emotional reactions when preparing for—or experiencing—a separation from a close friend, family member, or a special location.

● experiencing nightmares prior to, during, or following the breakup

You may have separation anxiety from the people you love if you've experienced some traumatic events in the past, particularly if they involved the death of a close relative. Comparably, suppose you're the type of person who needs a while to get used to a new environment. In that case, you may find that leaving a familiar one behind increases your risk of developing separation anxiety.

Chapter 2: Women's Social Anxiety

Both men and women suffer from social anxiety, but it appears to afflict women more than males. Additionally, several things make women more anxious than men. We will learn the reasons for the effects of social anxiety on women in this chapter.

Factors Affecting Women's Anxiety

Women may experience anxiety at higher rates for a variety of reasons. Let's review a few of the most significant ones.

Genetics's Function

Although certain genes that may cause social anxiety disorder have not yet been identified, experts generally agree that genetics plays a part in the onset of social anxiety disorder. Studies show that genetics account for over one-third of the causes of social anxiety. This is sometimes referred to as your social anxiety disorder's heritability. Furthermore, you have a far increased chance of acquiring social anxiety disorder if a first-degree relative—that is, your parent, child, or full sibling—has the condition (Cuncic, 2021).

It's important to remember that you may overcome your social anxiety symptoms even if your genes contribute to it. Don't let that be a justification for thinking that "This is just how I'm wired" and succumb to your habits.

Anxiety in Social Settings and the Environment

Here's an intriguing distinction between environmental and genetic factors: Our surroundings directly influence our behaviors more than our genes, even if genes can have a long-term impact on social anxiety symptoms. Environmental influences can also be transient, but certain experiences have a greater lasting effect than others. This is not to say that environmental influences are unimportant; rather, it is to say that they may be addressed over time. Of course, you might need some assistance to believe that you're more than the worst things that have occurred to you if you've had a traumatic incident that has severely affected you, such as years of bullying at school or abuse by a parent.

Our temperament is also inherited, so if we have low emotional stability or are prone to avoidant actions, our surroundings may significantly impact us. Therefore, our genes may also influence our innate responses to our surroundings.

Certain environmental elements have been found to have an impact on social anxiety. Traumatic life events, challenging peer relationships, emotional abuse, strict and judgmental parenting, and even other forms of abuse can all be detrimental to us (Norton & Abbott, 2017).

More recent studies have shown that physical abuse, loneliness, and bullying rank among the most significant psychosocial variables that might cause social anxiety disorder. However, the most socio-environmental factors contributing to this condition include a lack of parental and peer support (Khan & Khan, 2020).

Teenage Anxiety and the Brain

In terms of physical and emotional changes and the complex topography of the adolescent brain, the teenage years are a time of significant development. This chapter will take us on an exploration of the neuroscience of anxiety, the changes in the teenage brain during development, and the important role hormones play in defining the adolescent experience.

Section 1: The Development of the Adolescent Brain

It is essential to appreciate this developmental process in order to understand how anxiety can appear in the adolescent brain.

The concept of neuroplasticity Adolescents have exceptionally flexible brains capable of learning and evolving. Teenagers' neuroplasticity makes them quick learners of new information and abilities.

Frontal Lobe Formation: Throughout adolescence, the frontal lobes, which control impulse, emotion, and decision-making, undergo a lot of change. However, because of this unequal growth, there is a chance for impulsivity and emotional instability.

Peer Influence: There is a strong correlation between brain growth and the need for social acceptability and peer approval. Social relationships are important since adolescence is a time when the brain's reward system is most active.

Knowing the dynamic changes taking place in the adolescent brain can help explain why adolescents are more prone to anxiety and show how therapies can be customized to meet their specific developmental needs.

Section 2: Anxiety's Neurobiology

Anxiety is primarily a brain neurobiological phenomenon. It is not just a psychological experience. Analyzing the brain's contribution to anxiety aids in our understanding of its significant effects on adolescence.

The Amygdala: The brain's tiny, almond-shaped amygdala is a key component in processing emotions, especially fear and anxiety. In people with anxiety disorders, it can become hyperactive, which can cause elevated emotional reactions.

The amygdala and the prefrontal cortex work together to modulate emotional reactions. The prefrontal cortex controls executive processes like impulse control and decision-making. This circuitry's dysregulation may be a factor in anxiety.

Neurotransmitters: Dopamine and serotonin are two examples of the chemical messengers known as neurotransmitters that are important in anxiety. These neurotransmitter imbalances have the potential to impact mood and exacerbate anxiety symptoms.

Brain Circuits: Certain brain circuits responsible for stress response and threat detection are linked to anxiety. Those who suffer from anxiety disorders may develop hypersensitivity to these circuits.

The neurobiology of anxiety sheds light on this complicated disorder and emphasizes the need to treat neurological as well as psychological issues while treating and supporting teenagers with anxiety.

Section 3: The Function of Hormones

Adolescence is characterized by hormonal changes, which have a significant impact on the teen brain and the feeling of anxiety.

Hormonal Surge and Puberty: The onset of puberty results in several substantial hormonal changes, including. These modifications may impact emotional control and mood.

Stress Hormones: A normal reaction to stimuli is the release of stress hormones like cortisol. On the other hand, persistent worry and stress can cause these hormones to become dysregulated, which can exacerbate anxiety disorders.

Differences in Gender: Different genders experience different hormonal changes during adolescence, which may account for differences in the frequency and manifestation of anxiety disorders. Comprehending these distinctions is essential for customized methods of managing worry.

Hormones and Development of the Brain: The adolescent brain is partly shaped by hormones. Hormones and brain development interact to affect anxiety susceptibility and emotional reactions.

Understanding how hormones affect anxiety is crucial to comprehending the particular difficulties that teens confront during this developmental period. It also emphasizes how important it is to handle anxiety holistically, taking into account psychological and hormonal aspects.

Techniques and strategies for managing one's thoughts are covered in Chapter 5.

We have now reached the fifth and final chapter of this second book. My intellectual efforts will focus on answering several difficult questions in this final chapter. This chapter mostly offers helpful tips and directions regarding tactics you can learn to use.

Negative ideas frequently have hazardous cascading consequences, whereby one bad thought quickly follows another, causing the person to experience negative and detrimental outcomes. Preventing the negative issues from happening in the first place is the best way to ensure that this cascade effect never happens. This topic is covered in the chapter's second paragraph as well. It can take a while and be difficult to stop thinking negatively, but the effort is always worthwhile.

Lastly, I'll walk you through five helpful strategies for stopping the flow of thoughts—especially the flow of negative thoughts—using examples and helpful hints. Let's get straight to the first problem.

What does it mean to have mental control?

When we refer to "thought control," we can have two distinct meanings. One can speak of mental trickery on the one hand. This approach is regrettably quite common, yet it raises serious ethical issues. Regretfully, manipulation comes in many forms, and humans are readily molded. But this idea also has a more optimistic connotation. Self-control in thought can also apply to oneself. This paragraph aims to explain the beneficial aspects of thought regulation. Together, let's examine the critical processes involved in developing mental self-control.

Being conscious of one's mental patterns is the first step towards managing one's thoughts. One cannot be aware of one's virtues or shortcomings without awareness! Two things require awareness: First, one must be conscious of negative and dysfunctional thinking. Changing negative thought patterns requires taking this important step. But it's equally important to recognize one's strengths. Since our minds are our biggest tool, the more self-aware you are of your thoughts, the better equipped and more powerful you will be to live a life free from worry. Knowing oneself, though, is insufficient. Additionally, you need to be able to deliberately interfere with your thoughts' ability to govern them.

Two key components are involved in thought control. Having become aware and conscious, you must first develop the ability to block bad thoughts (I will go into more detail about this idea in the following paragraph); you must also develop the ability to generate positive thoughts. Your attitude toward the outside world must change, even though external events might remain the same. You won't be able to master 100% of your ideas until you cultivate an optimistic outlook. Set aside your pessimism and alter your perspective and, most importantly, how you respond to external circumstances. This is the crucial component for managing your thoughts!

You can continue reading to find out how to stop your negative ideas now that you know what it means to manage your mind. If you want to quit overanalyzing things, do this!

How do we stop thinking bad thoughts?

It would sound impressive to stop bad ideas with just your thinking! But rest assured, it is a workable solution. Together, let's examine some fundamental aspects of this problem.

Finding the internal or external factors that cause intrusive negative thoughts is the first step in blocking negative thoughts. If you do not first learn to identify what causes you to feel awful and generates negative thoughts, you will not be able to stop them from starting. As such, you must demand great sincerity from yourself: don't tell yourself falsehoods, and be forthright about what causes you pain and obsessive thought patterns.

Proceed to the "processing negative thoughts" stage after that. Why do some things or emotions cause you such pain?

For what reason does facing failures make you feel anxious? Maybe there were times when you could have stopped some bad things from happening, and you didn't act sooner. That might be a sort of guilt in this instance. In other situations, you could feel resentment toward someone, even if it's just subliminally. But remember that rage is one of those "invasive" emotions that can seep into every corner of your emotional realm. You will, therefore, grow to despise even yourself more the more hostile you are toward the foreigner. In summary, naming your feelings is crucial to preventing negative ideas. Once more, a great deal of sincerity is required.

Lastly, you should know that peace is the greatest defense against intrusive and negative ideas. This is before we go on to my useful advice on how to block negative thoughts. If you can achieve serenity, no negative idea can pierce your shield of optimism and positivity. Ultimately, the most crucial action to avoid overthinking and block out negative thoughts is to shift your perspective!

Now that you are aware of these crucial details, you can effectively prevent negative thoughts. But I want to dedicate more room to this crucial subject. As a result, I'll go over five methods in the following part to help you master thought control.

How to Get Serenity by Sleeping

We all know how important sleep is, but we frequently give it up first. *Fitful sleep* is a national problem brought on by stress, electronics, and work obligations. However, getting enough good sleep is essential to reducing worry. Consider sleep the foundation of your body; if it breaks, the entire building will sway.

Establish a regular sleep routine to start with the fundamentals. To stabilize your circadian rhythm. Maintaining a schedule encourages your body to anticipate and desire sleep. Invest in supple, breathable bedding to optimize comfort. Ensure that your room is quiet, cold, and fully dark. Earplugs, blackout curtains, and white noise apps can all be useful.

Establish a soothing evening routine to help your sympathetic nervous system into a resting state before going to bed. Dim the lights, read a book, take a warm bath, or listen to soothing music. Stay away from screens for one to two hours before bed. Blue light and mental activity prevent melatonin generation, making it more difficult to fall asleep.

Your exercise and food also impact sleep. Steer clear of large meals, coffee, and alcohol right before bed. Excessive exercise at night can overstimulate you, whereas exercise during the day is helpful. After 20 minutes in bed, if you haven't fallen asleep, get up, attempt to get some vital activity until you feel sleepy, and then go back to bed. This keeps you from connecting frustration with your bed.

Try journaling to help you get rid of worry or ruminating, or try a guided meditation to help you stay in the now. A weighted blanket, earplugs, a sleep mask, or blackout curtains can all help you get a better night's sleep. Maintaining good sleep hygiene gradually increases resilience, just like regular meditation.

Let's now go more deeply into particular methods for maximizing each stage of your sleep cycle:

Complete Your Evening

- One to two hours before bed, finish using and storing electronic devices.
- Turn down the lights, turn on calming music, and avoid news or conversations too close to home.
- Engage in soothing pursuits such as reading fiction.
- Take a sip of lavender or chamomile tea and practice guided breathing techniques.

Enhance Your Sleep Environment

- Make use of breathable, cozy bedding, such as supportive mattresses, light blankets, and soft sheets.
- If necessary, wear an eye mask and blackout curtains to keep your bedroom dark.

- Use a fan to create ambient background sound.
- Maintain a cold bedroom—ideally, no more than 65°F, as this will help your body regulate its temperature.

Maintain a Calm Evening Routine

- Establish soothing routines, such as putting on pajamas, turning down the lights, and setting an alarm to tell your brain when it's time to relax.
- To avoid being awakened by thoughts and to-do lists, write them down. Prepare for the following day.
- Since screens block melatonin, read a fiction book or magazine unconnected to your job or the news.

Make Your Mind Clear

- Steer clear of clock-watching and self-criticism, as these behaviors trigger stress hormones.
- To help you eliminate worried thoughts, write them down for ten minutes.
- Consider participating in a guided meditation where the goal is to calm your entire body, head to toe.

Take Supplements Carefully

See your physician before taking supplements, such as L-theanine, magnesium, valerian root, or melatonin.

- For a few weeks at most, take the lowest effective dose of melatonin (0.5–3 mg) two hours before bed to prevent reliance.

- Take 200–400 mg of L-theanine and magnesium one hour before bed.

Ask for More Help If You Need It

- Consult your physician about any underlying medical disorders that may be treated, such as sleep apnea, restless legs syndrome, or persistent pain.
- If over-the-counter remedies aren't enough for short-term use, talk to your doctor about prescription sleep aid choices.

Although it can be difficult, prioritizing good sleep hygiene and making it a non-negotiable practice will greatly impact your mental and general welfare. Practice self-compassion and prioritize progress over perfection. Sweet dreams!

You can get skilled at identifying skewed ideas before worry gets out of control. Change your thinking to make it more precise, adaptable, and solution-focused. You are in charge of your thoughts; they do not control you.

- Put up pictures of loved ones and special locations as visual cues to be grateful.

The more you practice gratitude, the more it compounds. Continue developing your ability to recognize and value all of life's blessings. When gratitude is your only focus, worrying is difficult.

Anxiety is worse when people are alone. Take care of your community and relationships by avoiding negativity and embracing positivity. Joy shared is joy multiplied. You don't need to face life by yourself.

How does Ha breathe?

The origin of Ha breathing is Ancient Hawaii. It is an easy and efficient method of relieving tension. The first syllable in Hawaiian is ha, which indicates breath. Translated, "Supreme life force that rides on the breath" is what Hawaii signifies.

Why Is Do Ha Inhaling?

Given the frenetic nature of today's society, everyone could likely use a stress-relieving tool that is simple to modify for usage in both public and private situations. You will soon find Ha breathing is very practical and easy to adopt into your daily life, no matter where or when you are.

I begin Session 1 by leading clients through Ha breathing when I work with them one-on-one in my coaching and hypnosis practice. From then on, Ha forms the cornerstone of all we do, including goal-setting, emotional baggage release, guided visualization, breaking bad habits, changing beliefs, and much more.

What Is It Exactly?

When we breathe in through our noses for four counts and out of our mouths for eight counts, we do Ha breathing. One characteristic distinguishing Ha's breathing is the expiration through the mouth, which is twice as long as the intake through the nose. We can more easily enter the parasympathetic nervous system's calm state by exhaling more air than we are taking in.

According to the Cleveland Clinic1, the parasympathetic nervous system regulates your body's short-term survival instincts and aids in relaxation during tranquil moments.

It's acceptable to choose a lesser total length if you cannot sustain the breathing pattern of four seconds in and eight seconds out, or 12 seconds overall. Three seconds in and six seconds out, for instance. Just maintain this 1:1:2 ratio.

Promoting diaphragmatic breathing is an often neglected advantage of practicing Ha breathing regularly.

Instead of breathing from their diaphragms, many people prefer to breathe via their mouths. Continuous mouth breathing, even while you're asleep, can cause complications.

Children who mouth breathe may have crooked teeth, facial abnormalities, or stunted growth. Chronic mouth breathing in adults can lead to gum disease and foul breath. It may also make the symptoms of other diseases worse.2. Breathing through your mouth can produce a dry mouth, which reduces saliva production, which can remove bacteria from the mouth and promote the growth of bacteria on the tongue, which causes a bad smell.3.

There are several advantages to diaphragmatic breathing that can impact your whole body. Because of this, it is a typical feature of many relaxation and meditation practices, which can reduce stress, blood pressure, and other vital body processes.4

Reducing stress is one of the main advantages of diaphragmatic breathing. Stress inhibits the immune system's ability to function at its best. You may become more prone to certain illnesses as a result. Even seemingly insignificant annoyances like traffic can occasionally cause long-term or chronic stress, which can result in anxiety or depression.5.

Even though Ha breathing is easy to comprehend and practice, my clients would benefit even more if I gave them a way to gauge its efficacy. In the context of our work, having a measurable sense of ease from the outset (with a simple self-help technique) fosters the confidence that more good improvements are ahead. You can see how crucial Ha breathing is to their success in getting the outcomes they want because our thoughts tend to become self-fulfilling prophesies. According to an old proverb, "Everything begins with the breath."

To support my customers' achievement even more, they must perceive Ha breathing as simple to practice independently in any setting, including stressful family situations, high-stakes business meetings, and foreign travel. For this reason, I introduced variants to Ha breathing and presented measures with Ha breathing. With these modifications, my clients can customize Ha's breathing to fit into any situation that comes their way. When individuals realize that the rapid outcomes they've already attained may be repeated in different situations, they start to feel more in control of their lives.

Anxiety's Effects on the Body

Anxiety causes your body to shake like it's at a surprise party. Your heart beats like a music video star—a dance-off without your permission. In your stomach, butterflies fly, making it a haven for nervous feelings. Your muscles tense up and become the marionettes of anxiety. Anxiety's puppeteer-like hold takes over, hunching the shoulders and stiffening the neck, making relaxation a distant memory.

Depression's Effects on Your Body

Depression and anxiety can seriously harm your health; they're not merely games played on your body. It's like raising a red flag if you observe these party crashers remaining for an extended period. Your body deserves more; this isn't just a temporary state. Therefore, don't be timid; ask for assistance, reach out, and eject those intruders. Anxiety and despair are not invited to the ultimate house party that your body, mind, and happiness deserve. You possess the ability to regain control and assert your authority over them!

Depression-Related Events

● Loss and grief: Have you ever had the impression that a ton of bricks were pressing down on your heart? That is the result of loss and grief. It seems to play a depressing melody nonstop in your head. Your emotions are filled with a symphony of pain that is created by memories and longing. It's acceptable to cry freely as if rainfall washed away the grief. Remember that in this emotional orchestra, you are not alone;

innumerable others have performed the same melody of grief.

● tension: Visualize tension as an abrupt tornado that rips through your mind, uprooting everything in its path and transforming it into a tranquil landscape. Stress can create a tumultuous whirl in your thoughts and emotions. It's like balancing too many balls simultaneously as riding an endless rollercoaster. Remember, nevertheless, that you are not helpless against this storm. You possess an inner strength umbrella. Gaining the ability to manage stress can act as a shield, enabling you to escape the chaos and take a break. You can withstand life's turbulence in the same way that a lighthouse does in a storm.

- Rejection: Imagine rejection as a heavyweight fighter hitting you in the confidence department. It's the depressing sense of not fitting in and being abandoned. Think of it like a difficult level in a video game where you might get briefly knocked out, but here's the secret: You have more lives than you need. Your entire journey is not defined by one rejection. It's only a diversion, a brief misstep on your journey. You can rise stronger and more determined than before, much like a phoenix does from the ashes. Recall that you are a work of art that is constantly evolving and that a single brushstroke does not determine the entire canvas.

● Life transitions and changes: These events are similar to embarking on a new route without knowing where it will go. It feels like you've stumbled into an enigmatic, winding maze you've never been in before. Navigating through fog can be how these shifts feel because of the uncertainty they bring with them. The truth is, though, you already possess a compass. Accepting change can open up fascinating new chapters, even if you're tiptoeing into the unknown. Every turn can lead to surprises and treasures, like an explorer embarking on a huge adventure. Thus, although the fork in the path may appear intimidating, it also opens the door to amazing prospects.

- Rationality: Have you ever had a mental block similar to an unstoppable song? That's your kind of ruminating. It's similar to going over and over in a movie scene, analyzing every little detail until your mind goes into overdrive. Like a hamster on a wheel, it spins but doesn't go anywhere. The point is, though, that you're not merely observing. The remote control is with you. You can halt, get off the thought loop, and change your mental channel. You own the remote control; your mind is your realm.
- Money problems: Imagine yourself strolling along a sandy beach when, all of a sudden, the sand turns into quicksand with each stride. Financial problems can sometimes feel like a bottomless pit of

anxieties. That persistent bug worries about finances, costs, and the future. Hold on, though—you're not alone. Think of your mind as an advanced calculator. You may subtract stress, add up the options, and perhaps even break your difficulties into smaller manageable pieces. Remember that asking for assistance is like using a lifeline in the game of life; it's not a sign of weakness.

● Abuse of substances: Abuse of substances can be compared to applying a band-aid to a wound that requires medical attention. It's like a getaway vehicle from the rough landscape of reality. The fact is, though, that you're more than just an escape artist. You are a fighter. You can direct your strength in more constructive directions rather than running for short-term safety. It feels like becoming a superhero instead of just a sidekick.

Depression triggers may attempt to infiltrate your narrative, but ultimately, you are the author. Recognizing their impact is akin to deciphering hidden meanings, directing you toward recovery and development. You are the story's protagonist; despite these obstacles, your story is one of bravery and success.

Handling Setbacks

Let's explore the wealth of techniques that can guide you through the challenging process of overcoming anxiety and depressive causes.

Observation and Deep Inhalation

Think of your breath as a stabilizing anchor in turbulent waters. When the triggers come, pause and concentrate on your breathing. Breathe in deeply and out slowly until you reach the count of six. Finding serenity in the middle of a storm can be achieved by practicing mindfulness and deep breathing.

Restructuring Cognitively

Imagine that your mind is a house that is being renovated. Restructuring your cognitive processes is akin to redesigning them. Provide evidence to refute negative thoughts that are triggered by triggers. By asking yourself, "Is this thought based on facts or assumptions?" you may redesign your mental landscape using a more grounded plan. It's like becoming your thought architect.

Expression of the Creative

Have you ever attempted writing, dancing, or painting? Giving your emotions a secure playground is similar to what creative expression is. Create art with your emotions when they arise. It's similar to crafting a masterpiece out of emotional pain. Allow your artistic expression to serve as a conduit between your healing process and your triggers.

Social Assistance

Visualize your friends and family as emotional support systems. Speak with them when the triggers go off. It's similar to calling in a backup support team. Talking to someone who can relate to your emotions can help you feel less alone and provide new insights.

Rhythm and Form

Consider your routine a handy safety net when unexpected events threaten to throw you off. Make a daily plan that includes things you enjoy doing. It's similar to building a strong base for your mental health. Having a schedule might help one feel stable and predictable when triggers occur.

Outdoors and Exercise

Think of nature as your mental refresh button. When triggers arise, take a stroll, a hike, or just relax outside. It has the effect of wiping off negativity with clean air. Engaging in physical activity helps you counteract the effects of triggers by releasing feel-good chemicals in your brain.

Good Night's Sleep

Imagine that sleep is a wonderful concoction that helps you mentally refresh. Remember that a restful night's sleep is your best defense against the impacts of triggers when they interfere with your sleep. Restful sleep makes your mind more capable of managing difficulties. Your resilience is strengthened by sleep, which makes it more difficult for triggers to negatively impact your emotions. Thus, remember that a restful night's sleep is your hidden weapon, making you resilient and prepared to handle any challenge that may arise when triggers interfere with your sleep.

6. Drug Abuse

A dangerous route into addiction, substance misuse has a severe negative effect on mental health in addition to physical health, serving as a cause and trigger for anxiety.

It's a convoluted and frequently terrifying road, where drugs that provide momentary comfort can turn into the chains that keep people trapped in the never-ending grip of dread.

Substances like alcohol, narcotics, or even prescription prescriptions may seem like a short-term solution to the problems of everyday living. They can give a false relief sensation, momentarily masking problems or emotional suffering. But the comfort is fleeting, and the following tension is frequently unrelenting.

The delicate chemical equilibrium of the brain can be upset by substance misuse. This chemical disruption can cause a crippling withdrawal process when anxiety becomes a daily companion, in addition to amplifying anxiety symptoms.

In addition, addiction can have a vicious cycle. People who use drugs may suffer a rebound effect, in which their anxiety returns stronger than before when the benefits wear off. This feeds the cycle of misuse by creating a desperate demand for more of the drug to relieve the worry.

Anxiety is brought on by both the pharmacological effects and the aftereffects of substance misuse. Financial hardship, marital difficulty, legal issues, and health issues frequently accompany addiction. These outside pressures provide an ideal environment for anxiety to grow, burdening sufferers with both emotional distress and outside chaos.

The close relationship that exists between substance abuse and anxiety serves as a sobering reminder of the devastation that addiction may cause. It's a complicated dance in which drugs, which at first provide an escape from emotional torment, eventually turn into the cause of even more misery. Gaining insight into this relationship is essential for those looking to heal and rehabilitate.

In the story of substance abuse as the source and catalyst for anxiety, empathy and assistance are critical components. The fact that addiction frequently conceals underlying mental health issues and emotional suffering emphasizes the necessity of all-encompassing addiction treatment programs that take care of a patient's emotional and physical needs.

In the end, the process of recovering from substance abuse is evidence of how resilient people can be. It's a path that entails freeing oneself from the bonds of addiction and regaining a life characterized by hope, healing, and revitalized well-being while negotiating the rough seas of worry.

7. Drugs

Contrary to popular belief, medications can paradoxically create and exacerbate anxiety in certain people. They are frequently thought of as the remedy to numerous maladies. The quest for improved health can take an intricate and unanticipated turn at times since the things meant to cure can occasionally create new difficulties on the physical and mental levels.

Medication side effects are one aspect of this intricate interaction. Several medications, including various stimulants, antidepressants, and even over-the-counter pharmaceuticals, can cause symptoms that are similar to anxiety. These could include an elevated level of agitation, a fast heartbeat, or restlessness. These side effects may feel like an unwanted intrusion to someone already prone to anxiety, which will exacerbate their mental suffering.

Furthermore, worry may be sparked by the fear of possible negative consequences. People may have anxiety when taking medicine because they are concerned about potential side effects or whether it will make their anxiety worse. This fear may start a vicious cycle of increased anxiety related to taking medications.

In some circumstances, anxiety may also arise during the process of reducing or stopping a particular medicine. It can be difficult to manage the underlying problem while also considering the possible side effects of drug modifications when dealing with withdrawal or discontinuation symptoms, which can include anxiety, among other impacts.

In these cases, a thorough discussion between the patient and their healthcare professional is essential because the advantages of the medication frequently exceed any possible negative effects.

Knowing that drugs can both induce and provoke anxiety emphasizes the importance of providing individualized, comprehensive treatment.

Medication can be a crucial part of the complex fabric of mental health, helping to reduce pain. However, it serves as a reminder that everyone needs different medical treatment and that each person may react differently to certain drugs. It emphasizes how crucial it is to monitor patients, modify care as necessary, and support people navigating the complex mental health and medicine world.

These illnesses, which are hidden and feed on vulnerability and fear, destroy mental health and take over people's lives. It's important to realize, though, that you don't need to wait for a traumatic incident to get support and look after your mental health. For instance, therapy helps you build positive ideas and behaviors in your head, much like going to the gym does.

Charles's mental health was critically ill when his family ultimately decided to seek professional assistance. They were unaware of the profound effects that anxiety and depression may have on a person's life, much like a lot of other families. But in order to start the healing process and comprehend these illnesses better, this step was essential.

Prior to beginning treatment, Charles struggled alone with his inner demons, unable to find a way to release tense muscles, sleeplessness, and a persistent sense that something awful was going to happen. His old skating buddies showed up one day while he was stuck at home thinking nothing but bad things, and they invited him to hang out and watch them practice their feats.

Charles accepted the invitation, acknowledging that his mother had most likely planned this to get him out of the room where he spent most of his time. Something weird happened as he was watching his friends enjoy themselves while sitting outside. Everything went black instantly, leaving him with his companions' slow-motion antics and smiles to keep him company. That's when the notion that would destroy him like a nuclear bomb struck him: "You'll never be able to skate again."

Charles experienced a pivotal moment when he realized his life would never be the same. He felt even more empty inside at the idea that he would never be able to skate again, which fueled the worry and despair plaguing him for so long. After experiencing such great loss, he went back to his room and sobbed for days, unable to find a cause to move on.

His mother became concerned for his mental health after observing that he had regressed and decided to consult a psychologist. Charles' life took a drastic change after making this choice. He started seeing Leo, the psychologist, at home once a week. Charles was quiet and reclusive at first, but he progressively revealed more over the sessions and shared his worries with Leo.

Three individuals provided crucial support throughout this journey: his mother, Terezinha, who never gave up on him; Daniela, the physiotherapist who assisted with his physical recovery; and Leo, the psychologist who led him through therapy. Together, they were essential to Charles's journey of recovery because he yearned for an end to the suffering, fear, and anguish that anxiety and depression had brought into his life.

Charles started to have a different outlook on life after attending multiple therapy sessions. He changed from being someone who didn't think it was worth living to someone courageous and determined to take on the challenges of this new stage of life. Her bond with the physiotherapist Daniela also grew, and they became wonderful, confiding friends. Meanwhile, all the other pals from his day had moved on.

Charles realized that in order to escape the pit that his episodes of anxiety and despair had dug him into, he had to take the assistance that was being provided to him. As time passed, he was given a unique present on his thirteenth birthday: the tiny muscle of his left thigh started reacting to stimuli. He had not moved from the waist down until then, so this improvement was noteworthy and worthy of celebration.

This historic event signaled a sea change in his life and demonstrated the fearlessness of his goals. He decided to take a different approach to life, giving up on being the victim of his circumstances and taking control of his narrative. Charles hit the "turbo button" in his mental evolution, speeding up and significantly altering this new phase of his life.

Charles continued his rehabilitation without complaint, thinking only about the good things he may accomplish. He continued seeing the psychologist and receiving physiotherapy, adding hydrotherapy to his regimen. He thought about Ecotherapy, a method of working on balance that entailed riding a horse, but ultimately gave up since he feared being seen on the neighborhood's streets.

His mental and physical development was beneficial over time. He stopped thinking negatively about ending his life and started interacting with people more easily. The sense that his time was running out vanished as he learned to manage his anxieties and panic episodes and overcame the ideas that made him feel helpless and weak.

Charles was determined to attempt using a walker once his hip strength started to increase. But as time passed, he understood that his family's wishes drove him more than his desires. He started to wonder if he wanted to regain his mobility or if it was more of a desire held by others.

He found it quite challenging because he was unable to execute every movement. Using the strength of his arms, he crawled while supporting his body. Furthermore, he experienced soreness in his leg following exercise that persisted the rest of the day due to regular activities. He was sick of being in constant agony and being caught in this bothersome loop that made it difficult for him to eat or sleep.

After a protracted period of this agonizing cycle, he was fully worn out and yearned for rest. Since only he understood the hardships of living in a wheelchair, he decided to give up on the challenge of walking again and accept his life as such. He was prepared to take on whatever was in store. He took control of his life and gave himself some consideration. She was no longer in pain, and her mental state was improving, so she started to focus on the good things.

After making that choice, Charles started to genuinely live for himself since he realized that only he could decide how far he could go. His mind led him to realize that he didn't have to walk to fulfill all of his dreams. He needed time in this new phase to figure out who he was and what he was ready to give up. As a wheelchair user, he was curious about his capabilities and restrictions. It was a time of building, self-discovery, and overcoming numerous previously unheard-of difficulties. Charles came to understand that boundaries are merely hypothetical during this procedure.

Charles decided to return to school and finish his education even though his weight and need for a wheelchair had damaged his self-esteem. After high school, she enrolled in an administrative assistant course where she learned a few soft skills. He was responsible for starting and presenting a business to his peers during a monthly exam. Despite having just one coworker who was apprehensive about performing, he overcame his fear and completed the presentation by himself. Remarkably, the work was well accepted; the professor gave it accolades, and his classmates acknowledged him as creative.

Charles felt great enthusiasm and conviction that he could achieve anything he set his mind to at that moment. This concept had a strong hold on his thoughts. She began to think that she could make anything successful, whether in business or interpersonal relationships, just as he had come to think that the sky was blue. A little attitude was the beginning of it all.

Charles chose to pursue his business administration and psychology education after finishing his administrative assistant degree. She also purchased her vehicle and obtained her driver's license during this period. She also decided to take on the role of micro franchisee and managed a sizable staff. He was able to address over 300 individuals about business on a single platform. Charles decided to live alone after moving out of his parent's home to further push himself. Charles experienced a dramatic emotional and physical metamorphosis and gained recognition as resilient and a reputation for kindness.

Charles realizes he is truly strongest when forced to use his strength. Charles decided to move on and pretend that nothing had occurred. Charles changed his life by facing his worries and going forward without looking back in an attempt to feel more and more alive. During her voyage, she understood that life is the world's largest company and that only it can prevent it from going out of business. He also realized that finding love in the chaos of life, fortitude in the face of adversity, and optimism in the face of storms, falls, or disappointments makes one happy, not the absence of these things. One must consider past grievances, draw lessons from adversity, and discover happiness in isolated times to be happy. Being joyful is taking control of one's narrative and realizing that life is worthwhile despite obstacles and crises.

ASSISTING YOUR AUTISM-SUFFERING CHILD TO LIVE

You may have many questions. Uncertainty and fear may accompany the diagnosis; no parent is ever ready to hear such news. You could be perplexed by the range of therapy options available, or you might not know how best to help your child. While ASD is not something that a child can outgrow, it's important to keep in mind that there are a variety of therapies and resources available to support children in learning new abilities and overcoming developmental obstacles.

The special needs of kids with ASD can be met by a range of options, including in-home behavioral therapy, government services, and school-based initiatives. These tools can aid your child's development and growth and provide them with a fulfilling life.

It's also critical that you look after yourself as you care for your autistic child. You may be the greatest parent you can be for your child by keeping your emotional fortitude intact. Having an autistic child can be easier to manage with this parenting advice.

Act Now, Even in the Event of No Diagnosis

It's critical to act right away if you think your child may have an ASD or developmental delays associated with it. It is not a good idea to wait to see if your child outgrows the problem or catches up. Not even waiting for a formal diagnosis is appropriate. For children with autism spectrum conditions, early intervention is essential since it greatly improves the likelihood of a favorable outcome. Early intervention can help your child grow more quickly and experience fewer lifetime symptoms of autism.

Comprehending Autism in Your Child

Develop Your Knowledge of Your Child

Determine what prompts your child to engage in difficult or disruptive behaviors and what elicits favorable reactions from them. Recognize whether circumstances make your child feel anxious, scared, at ease, uncomfortable, or joyful. This information will assist you in resolving issues and avoiding or adjusting to challenging circumstances.

Accept Your Child's Individuality

Practice acceptance instead of focusing on how your autistic child is different from other kids and what they might be "missing." Celebrate your child's little victories, enjoy their unique characteristics, and avoid comparing them to other kids. Your youngster will gain more from unconditional love and acceptance than anything else.

Remain Resilient

The course of autism spectrum disease is unpredictable. Refrain from assuming anything about your child's future too soon. just like everyone else. Remain upbeat and never stop encouraging your youngster on their path.

First tip: Create a supportive atmosphere for your autistic child.

It's essential to give your autistic child safety and stability in their everyday lives if you want them to flourish. To help you and your kid with ASD manage life at home, think about implementing the following strategies in addition to learning about autism and receiving treatment:

1. Stability Is Essential: It can be difficult for kids with ASD to transfer their knowledge from one context to another. Use strategies from your child's treatment sessions to establish consistency in their surroundings.

Encourage therapy in numerous locations to encourage the transfer of abilities between environments. Maintaining consistency in your interactions and your approach to difficult habits is crucial.

2. Adhere to a Schedule: Schedules or routines that are structured are beneficial for children with autism. Make a daily plan that includes set hours for eating, therapy, school, and sleeping. if a schedule adjustment is necessary, let your child know beforehand.

3. Reward Positive Behavior: When it comes to kids with ASD, positive reinforcement works wonders. Reward and commend them when they behave well or pick up new abilities. Give

particular examples of the behaviors you find admirable. Think about rewarding them with stickers or letting them play with a favorite toy instead of just one.

4. Establish a Safe Space: Give your child a haven where they may unwind and feel protected. Ensure this area is set up and your child understands the boundaries. Visual cues can be useful. Examples include labeling goods with pictures or using colored tape to denote off-limits locations. Childproof your house if needed, particularly if your youngster has tantrums or engages in self-harming activities.

These techniques can help your autistic child thrive and develop by creating a loving and supportive atmosphere.

The Activating Event, Belief, and Consequence (ABC) Model of CBT

Dissecting the ABCs

Learning the fundamental grammar of your emotional language is similar to comprehending the Activating Event, Belief, and Consequence (ABC) Model in cognitive behavioral therapy. One of the pioneers of cognitive-behavioral therapies, Albert Ellis, created the model, a fundamental idea that enables you to analyze the structure of your emotions, behaviors, and thought processes.

Now let's explore what ABC represents:

The Activating Event Is the circumstance or event you encounter that initiates things. An internal trigger, such as a memory or bodily experience, or an external one, such as a colleague's remark, might be an activating event. It is vital to remember that the event is neutral in and of itself; your perspective adds color and emotional tone.

Belief: When you experience an activating event, your mind begins to analyze the event's significance for you. These convictions may or may not be reasonable. Cognitive distortions frequently taint irrational ideas, which can have negative emotional and behavioral effects that may not be in your best interests.

Consequence: This refers to the effects of your thinking on your actions and emotions. Your beliefs about the activating event shape how you feel and act.

Let's look at an example to help you better apply the ABC paradigm daily. Let's say you are presenting a presentation, and you see someone in the audience is dozing off (Activating Event). The thought that you're uninteresting and unworthy may quickly cross your thoughts (Belief). You might so experience anxiety and lose concentration, which could cause you to stumble through the remainder of your speech (Consequence).

The ABC approach doesn't stop here, though. Many specialists advise expanding it to the ABCDE model, in which E represents "Effective New Belief or New Experience" and D stands for "Disputing." You can create a path toward better feelings and actions by disputing and replacing your false beliefs with true ones (Effective New Beliefs or New Experiences).

The ABC paradigm encourages proactive questioning of illogical beliefs in addition to helping you understand your emotional reactions. It's the initial move toward rebuilding your mental model so you can respond to life's various circumstances more healthily.

Even though we've covered the fundamentals of CBT in this section, the true effectiveness of this model becomes apparent when you use it in the real world, particularly when faced with difficult emotions or choices. Using the ABC approach to analyze your experiences helps you understand your feelings and create a foundation for better, more positive thoughts and behaviors.

When the ABC model is completely embraced, it may be used as a diagnostic tool and a therapeutic pathway, giving you the tools you need to better understand yourself and deal with life's challenges with greater resilience and wisdom.

Useful Illustrations

Let's explore real-world examples of the ABC model's practical uses to make it more than just an abstract idea. The "real world" frequently offers less time and space for reflection, but therapeutic settings provide a safe area to examine your cognitive patterns. But the real strength of the concept is seen in how applicable it is outside of the therapist's office.

Individual Connections

Think of an argument with a close friend or relative. You may interpret something they say as an attack (Activating Event). Your first thought can be that you are disregarded or unloved (Belief). You might feel offended or enraged by this (Consequence). The problem is that you use the ABC model instead of responding to these feelings. You assess the trigger event and refute your assumption. Could their comment have been made for other reasons? Your emotional and behavioral reactions might become more restrained and productive once you refute and reframe your viewpoint. By doing this, you avoid strained relationships and gain emotional intelligence.

Interactions at Work

Suppose your supervisor gives you unfavorable criticism in a work environment (Activating Event). You may have started out thinking, "I'm incompetent" (Belief), which demoralized you (Consequence). You can analyze and challenge the validity of this chain by applying the ABC model. Is one negative comment enough to determine your value or level of expertise? One way to change the outcome from feeling defeated to being encouraged to improve is to reframe the mindset to something like "I have areas to improve, which is normal."

Stress and Taking Care of Oneself

Many times, stress leads to cognitive distortions. Assume for the moment that your workload is excessive (Activating Event). "I can't handle this; it's too much" (Belief) may be your innate belief. What was the outcome? Procrastination and even anxiety (Consequence). You can analyze this stress response with the use of the ABC model. Is it possible that you're exaggerating how dire things are? What if you divided jobs into smaller, more doable components? Stress can be turned into an action plan by refuting the illogical belief and forming a more useful belief.

The Basics of Making Decisions

The ABC model is essential for decision-making and helping comprehend emotional responses. Your beliefs can greatly influence your decisions about an occurrence. Your ultimate decision, for example, when considering a career shift, will be influenced by your perception of your skills and the associated dangers. By analyzing these beliefs using the ABC lens, You can ensure that your decisions are founded on logical assessments rather than cognitive distortions.

The ABC model's versatility is what makes it so lovely. You will find that this framework works for any situation, even though these examples are just for illustration purposes. It's like having a Swiss Army knife for your mind—you can use it in various situations to better analyze and comprehend your feelings, ideas, and behaviors. As you get better at applying the ABC model, you'll discover that it comes naturally to disprove false ideas and make room for more positive feelings and behaviors.

Exercise 12: Charts of Identity

Identity charts come in various forms, but they all assist you in examining the elements that make you who you are. They let you understand the components of your identity and your connections with those around you.

Before making your identity chart, You must first brainstorm several of your identities. You need to consider things like your place in your family, hobbies and interests, physical attributes, and history. Next, take a sheet of paper, write your name in the center, and list all your daily roles. For instance, you may be a brother or a sister, a Catholic or an atheist. You may have an intense interest in sports or literature. Even if you may be a US citizen, your relatives may be foreign-born. Studying hate science and English may be enjoyable for you. To understand who you are and what shapes your personality, list all the identities you can think of.

Three other versions of your identity chart are also possible to make. You can include how other people see you. To write down how you define yourself, draw arrows pointing out of the middle of the paper; to write down how other people see you draw arrows pointing into the center. There are situations when arrows may cross across, and your viewpoint aligns. This is an intriguing activity since it makes you aware of the differences between how you and other people see yourself.

Choosing the five elements you believe have had the greatest influence on who you are is one way to customize your identity chart. For instance, you might believe that while being a Catholic isn't vital to you, being a sister or brother is. Lastly, an identity chart that considers the various situations in your life and the elements that best represent who you are in each one can be made. Five factors come to mind that influence your identity in many contexts, such as school, family, friends, and so forth. Compared to the previous exercises, this one is more in-depth since it lets you examine any situation in which you have a significant impact.

Exercise 13: Methods for Grounding

Popular exercises known as "grounding techniques" assist people in letting go of negative sensations, memories, or flashbacks while concentrating on the here and now. As a result, they are quite helpful when depersonalization occurs. However, even if you don't have any of these conditions, you may still find them useful for reducing tension under trying circumstances. Grounding techniques are easy to practice and don't require any additional equipment or conditions. They are physical, mental, and relaxing.

Put another way, you can practice them anywhere and at any time. Physical grounding methods assist you in focusing on your body and induce physical relaxation. You could, for instance, submerge your hands in water and consider the feelings that arise. Additionally, you can use cold and warm water interchangeably. If not, you can interact with the objects around you by focusing on them. Examine their features, color, and shape, and feel them. Try describing the goods with as many specifics and technical terms as possible. Consuming food or beverages might aid in bringing your attention to the here and now while you eat or drink. You can choose foods or drinks that give you intense sensations to help make the activity simpler. Another simple physical grounding strategy is to move your body, which can be as simple as stretching or basic exercises. As you may have guessed, physical grounding techniques help you concentrate on your five senses: smell, touch, sight, hearing, and taste. Just consider inventive ways to engage your senses whenever you need to de-stress.

Mental grounding methods help you de-stress and divert your attention from tense situations. These consist of playing memory games, utilizing arithmetic and numbers, reciting, laughing, and keeping your mind occupied. For example, you could close your eyes, focus on a picture, and try to recall every image component. If not, you can count or label every object in the space or setting you're in that is that color. The more you can divert yourself from the task, the more difficult it is. As a result, counting allows you to multiply, divide, add, and subtract. Lastly, gentle grounding exercises encourage positive emotions. You can try to envision someone you love, close your eyes, and imagine their serene face and voice. If you own a pet or can readily obtain one, seize it and give it a firm embrace or stroke. People are always happier and more at ease around our furry buddies. Touching something reassuring generally helps bring you back to the present. If not, imagine a peaceful setting or arrange a quick activity you would like to accomplish.

The Effects of Anxiety and Stress

Anxiety and stress are more than just vague ideas that permeate our daily existence. They are real, potent forces that can influence our thoughts, feelings, and behaviors. We shall examine the significant effects that stress and anxiety can have on our wellbeing in this section.

Effects on the Body

Imagine your body as a well-tuned instrument, with every system and organ functioning in unison to sustain you. It's as though a discordant note has been added to this symphony of life when worry and anxiety enter the picture. These feelings have a wide range of physical repercussions.

Cardiovascular Health: The most important muscle in your body is your heart. Over time, stress can cause your heart to beat more forcefully and quickly, raising your risk of hypertension and heart disease. Your heart seems to be preparing for a marathon it never signed up for.

Muscle Tension: Have you ever noticed that your shoulders tend to sag towards your ears during stressful or nervous moments? This is only one illustration of how these feelings affect your muscles. Aches, pains, and even tension headaches can result from persistent tension.

Immune System: Your immune system is also negatively impacted by stress.

Your body's defenses are weakened, making you more vulnerable to infections ranging from minor ailments like the common cold to more serious ones.

Digestive Problems: Stress can cause stomach distress, which can aggravate illnesses like ulcers and cause problems like indigestion and irritable bowel syndrome (IBS).

Remain asleep when you're anxious, as anxiety can take over your sleep habits. Stress and worry can have a greater physical toll when insufficient sleep exists.

You may feel exhausted and ill due to the interconnectedness of these physical impacts, which are not separate occurrences. It's critical to interpret these bodily cues as a call to action.

Effects on the Emotions and Mind

Stress and worry have a profound effect on your thoughts and emotions in addition to your physical health.

Cognitive Function: Anxiety and stress can make it difficult for you to focus and make judgments.

Recollection: Have you ever had a "mental block" under pressure? This is a typical occurrence. Anxiety and stress can impair both short- and long-term memory, making it challenging to remember even the most basic information.

Mood Swings: These feelings can send your mood on a wild ride. You may start to experience mood fluctuations, irritability, and general uneasiness daily.

Depression: Prolonged worry and stress can be precursors of depression. A profound sense of hopelessness and sadness might result from ongoing stress on your mental health.

Behavioural Repercussions

Think of stress and anxiety as the directors calling the shots and your mind and body as actors on a stage. These directors have a big influence on how you act.

Procrastination: Anxiety and stress can cause you to put off important duties. It's possible to get caught up in an avoidance loop, which makes stress levels rise when deadlines approach.

Social Withdrawal: Social isolation can be a result of anxiety in particular. Due to this, you can become socially awkward or even start avoiding your friends and family.

Substance Abuse: Some people use drugs, alcohol, or other substances as a coping method for their stress and worry. This can exacerbate the issue by increasing the risk of addiction.

Changes in Eating Habits: Stress eating and appetite loss are two other behavioral reactions to these feelings that may result in unhealthful eating habits.

Regaining control over your life starts with realizing the consequences stress and anxiety have on your body, mind, and behavior. In the next chapters, we will look at methods and approaches to deal with each of these aspects in detail. You may reestablish harmony and balance in your body, mind, and behavior by learning to control and lessen these effects, leading to a happier and healthier version of yourself.

Taking Stock of the Present: A Path to Conscious Living

Have you ever been engulfed in a tornado of anxieties, obsessed with ideas about the past or the future? Women who are coping with anxiety problems frequently yearn for calm and connection. Introducing mindful living is a way of life that encourages us to live in the present and develops a better awareness of the outside world and ourselves. Together, let's go on this introspective trip to discover the amazing advantages of mindful living.

In its basic form, mindful living is a way of being that invites us to live in the present moment, completely aware of our feelings, thoughts, and environment, and free from distraction or judgment. Inspired by long-standing spiritual practices, it has acquired popularity recently because of its efficaciousness in reducing stress and anxiety.

By keeping us anchored in the now, mindfulness enables us to release the burden of the past and the uncertainty of the future. It can take many forms, from structured exercises like yoga and meditation to basic yet deep breathing exercises. A mindful way of life can be facilitated by even tiny changes to our everyday routines, such as setting up a short period each day to concentrate on breathing or enjoy the sensations of eating or walking.

We can learn to let go of the anxieties and concerns that frequently consume us by focusing on the here and now. Rather, we cultivate a state of serenity and acceptance of the events in our lives. Furthermore, practicing mindfulness can significantly improve our general mental health and wellbeing. Research has demonstrated that it can enhance happiness, promote contentment, cultivate more positive relationships, and even fortify our immune system.

The advantages of living thoughtfully are evident whether you investigate mindfulness meditation, start a yoga practice, or just try to be more present in your daily activities.

Chapter 2: Handling Emotional Difficulties

Love is an adventure with its special turns and turns. When ADHD travels with you, the journey can be thrilling as well as challenging. Managing the emotional terrain is one of the biggest challenges couples encounter when ADHD is present in their relationship patterns. Relationships use emotions as a color palette, and a calm and fulfilling relationship depends on understanding how ADHD affects this palette.

The Psychological Maze

The core of our human existence is our emotions. They mold our days, influencing our perceptions and interactions with the outside world. Emotions are the foundation for a partnership's connection, intimacy, and mutual understanding.

Strength and Unpredictability:

Feelings can become more intense and erratic as a result of ADHD. One might reach extremes of feeling, where happiness is euphoric, and rage crushes. An insignificant event might cause a wave of emotions akin to an unexpected track on a rollercoaster.

Selectivity to Rejection:

It is common for people with ADHD to exhibit rejection sensitivity. Real or imagined rejection can profoundly impact and elicit powerful feelings. It's similar to standing on a wire, where the crippling dread of falling occurs.

Impulsivity and Sensitivity to Feelings:

Impulsivity frequently results in quick emotional responses. Without a filter, a casual remark, a minor quarrel, or an unanticipated plan change might cause a rapid emotional reaction. It resembles a spark that ignites in a matter of seconds.

The Relationship Ripple Effect

When emotions are released into the calm waters of a relationship, they can create waves that travel great distances.

It's important to recognize these waves and develop coping mechanisms in order to comprehend the social difficulties that ADHD poses in relationships.

Effect on Interaction:

Emotions heavily influence conversation. It might be challenging to have a successful conversation when feelings are heightened and unstable due to ADHD. Misunderstandings may intensify, and the upheaval in feelings may obscure the actual intent behind the statements.

Promoting Compassion and Perception:

Handling emotional challenges requires great consideration and tolerance from both sides. The partner with ADHD may struggle to express and regulate their sentiments, while the partner without ADHD may find it difficult to understand the rush of emotions. It's a dance of kindness, patience, and sincerely attempting to walk in the other person's shoes.

Techniques for Handling Emotional Difficulties

Even though ADHD can lead to emotional upheaval, there are strategies that couples can employ to navigate these turbulent waters and arrive at more tranquil waters.

Putting Emotional Regulation Techniques into Practice:

Acquiring and utilizing techniques for managing emotions is crucial. These techniques can involve awareness exercises, calm breathing, or pausing briefly before answering. The trick is to figure out how to lower your mental volume when necessary.

Establishing a Secure Emotional Area:

Creating a secure space for emotional release should be a joint effort between the spouses.

This entails listening to one another without judgment, validating one another's emotions, and offering consolation and support. It's about establishing an environment where emotions are acknowledged and valued.

Couples therapy can provide a structured environment for discussing emotional difficulties, picking up coping mechanisms, and strengthening emotional bonds.

Making Self-Care a Priority:

The basis of mental health is personal self-care. Self-care techniques that assist in stress management, emotional balance, and maintaining a healthy emotional state should be valued by both partners.

The Emotional Dance: Fostering Bonding

The partners take the starring roles in the intricate ballet of emotions that is an ADHD-affected relationship. It's all about picking up the rhythm, matching the moves, and memorizing the routines.

Improving Emotional Bonding:

ADHD can, despite its challenges, build emotional bonds. A strong and profound friendship can be formed by sharing the ups and downs of life, learning to weather storms together, and celebrating the good days.

The Development of Emotional Intelligence

Emotional intelligence includes the capacity for both feeling and controlling emotions. Understanding triggers, learning to respond rather than react, and promoting mental growth in oneself and oneself as a pair are all part of the path.

It's important to comprehend the dance of feelings in order to manage the emotional difficulties that ADHD presents in a relationship. It's about accepting the vibrant kaleidoscope that emotions bring, understanding the specific effects of ADHD, and forging a bond that endures through emotional storms. Feelings become the threads that weave a lovely web of love and understanding in a relationship when they are acknowledged, understood, and handled with kindness and care.

Establishing Robust Connections:

- Develop wholesome, uplifting interactions with people in your vicinity. Resilience stems from having strong social ties.

- To keep relationships positive, practice good communication and conflict resolution techniques.

Keeping Things in Perspective:

- View the wider view to help you put difficulties into perspective. Acknowledge that hardships are a part of life and that you can overcome them.

Use your experiences to demonstrate your fortitude and capacity to manage trying circumstances.

Introspection

- Practice self-reflection regularly to understand your feelings, ideas, and actions.

- Journaling, mindfulness meditation, and therapy can be helpful resources for self-examination and self-awareness.

Acquiring Knowledge from Mistakes:

Accept setbacks and failures as chances for development and learning. Recognize that making errors is a necessary component of learning.

- Make use of failure as a springboard for success in the future.

Organising and Managing Time:

- Learn efficient time management techniques to lower stress and boost output. To reduce feeling overwhelmed, prioritize and arrange your duties.

Providing Assistance to Others:

- Show compassion and assistance to those who are in need. You may increase your resilience and wellbeing by being kind to and supporting others.

Resilience skill development is a continuous process that calls for self-compassion and practice. By honing these abilities, you'll be more capable of overcoming obstacles in life with bravery and hope, ultimately improving your mental and emotional health.

Sustaining an Equilibrium Way of Life

A balanced lifestyle is essential for general wellbeing because it enables people to reduce stress, enhance their physical health, and lead satisfying lives. Maintaining equilibrium among different facets of life can result in greater resilience, less stress, and happier living. Let's take a closer look at the essential elements of upholding a balanced lifestyle:

Making Self-Care a Priority:

- Self-care is making conscious decisions to look after your mental, emotional, and physical wellbeing. This covers things like eating healthily, sleeping enough, and working out regularly.

It's crucial to engage in self-compassion practices. Be gentle to yourself, just as you would a friend.

Work-Life Harmony:

It's critical to strike a healthy work-life balance to lower stress and preserve wellbeing.

- To prevent burnout, take regular pauses, use vacation time, and refrain from overworking.

Effective Time Management:

You can more effectively allocate time to many elements of your life by practicing efficient time management. Set priorities for your work so that you can give your family, your interests, and your downtime enough attention.

- Manage your time using calendars, to-do lists, and productivity tools.

Physical Condition:

- The cornerstones of physical health are proper sleep, a balanced diet, and regular exercise. Exercise is good for your physical, but it's also good for your mental and emotional wellbeing.

Steer clear of tobacco, alcohol, and other dangerous substances in excess.

Emotional and Mental Health:

- Take part in mental and emotional wellbeing exercises like journaling, mindfulness meditation, or counseling.

- Create coping mechanisms to handle stress and emotions efficiently.

Social Relations:

- Preserve positive social connections by keeping in touch with loved ones. Emotional health depends on social support.

- Foster connections using attentive listening, empathy, and meaningful exchanges.

Interests and Hobbies:

- Set aside time for activities and hobbies that make you happy and fulfilled. Doing something you enjoy gives you a sense of purpose and calm.

- Use artistic, musical, or literary endeavors as a vehicle for self-expression.

Having Enough Money:

Make prudent financial decisions by sticking to a budget, setting aside money for the future, and minimizing debt.

- Having a stable finance can bring comfort and less stress.

Religion and Mission:

Investigate your spirituality and look for a life's purpose. This could entail practicing mindfulness, religion, or introspection.

- You can feel more fulfilled when your activities align with your ideals.

You can see that these two descriptions—of shyness and social anxiety—share a lot of similarities. There is no denying this. But if you think of shyness and social anxiety as points on a spectrum, you can begin to understand their underlying distinctions. If so, shyness can be considered a far less severe form of social anxiety. Their symptoms may, therefore, be very similar, but the degree to which they are experienced varies greatly, and as a result, the behaviors that arise may also differ greatly. Therefore, while dread and anxiety may be experienced to some extent by shy people, these feelings typically do not lead to a lot of unhealthy habits and behaviors. These feelings nearly invariably cause them to engage in several maladaptive tactics and behaviors. Thus, the degree of avoidance, impairment of functioning, and severity of distress are the primary distinctions between social anxiety and shyness. Shy people feel less distressed, but not to the point that it interferes with their ability to operate normally. This implies that they are not guided to avoid any specific circumstance. High levels of distress that interfere with everyday living and prevent them from functioning normally are experienced by those who suffer from social anxiety. As a result, people start to avoid social interactions because they feel overpowering and frightening. A person suffering from social anxiety is not just going to feel uneasy before giving a speech (which is about as far along as symptoms from shyness go). A person who struggles with social anxiety could worry days or even weeks before the speech. Their body may experience physical symptoms of anxiety, such as sweating, trembling, racing heartbeats, insomnia, and shortness of breath. And as the crisis approaches, these symptoms might not go away but rather worsen. In this case, the person's concern might not go away, and they might suffer even after realizing their worries are unjustified or have no influence over the circumstance. Hence, even though shyness is a common sign of social anxiety, social anxiety is not necessarily experienced by shy people.

Recognising social anxiety, its warning signs, and its risks

Let's define social anxiety now that you know what it isn't. A persistent, crippling fear of social situations is known as social anxiety. This persistent, illogical worry can interfere with day-to-day activities, regular functioning, relationships, career, and education. While worrying before, during, and after social events is a common occurrence, social anxiety makes you worry all three of those times. Anxiety is not always a bad feeling; it's a common stress reaction. When the stressor has passed, but the worry persists, there is a problem. In cases of anxiety disorders, this is true. Eliminating the source of the stress does not lessen the feeling itself. This is the difference between experiencing anxiety and having anxiety. Anxiety is merely a stress response, and it usually doesn't have a major negative impact on your life or give you unnecessary emotional suffering. When an emotion starts to interfere with your life, it's called anxiety. Seeing it as a continuum will help you better understand the difference between anxiety and being nervous on the moderate end of the scale. This is an appropriate stress response.

On the end of this spectrum, anxiety occurs when your response is disproportionate to the circumstances and truly interferes with your capacity to operate normally. Thus, while worry could be useful in some circumstances, it also affects your ability to function in others. You should be conscious of your worry levels and start looking for support when it reaches this point. When faced with uncertainty, you will also display abnormal and excessive anticipatory behaviors, which is another sign that you need to get therapy for your anxiety. This implies that you can have unrealistic or out-of-reach expectations for the uncertainty and potential results. Furthermore, even though you have a legitimate cause for anxiety, you will experience excessive and persistent anxieties that refuse to go away.

Now that you are familiar with the term, let's look at a long list of symptoms so you can recognize the warning signals of social anxiety. The three primary types of symptoms are behavioral, emotional, and physical. These are the three ways that a person with social anxiety may present themselves. The person experiencing these symptoms finds it difficult to ignore or dismiss them due to their distinctiveness and uniqueness. Although they typically won't comprehend the depth and severity of the anxiety being felt, others may also detect that something is wrong with social anxiety sufferers. Social interactions may frequently cause a strong, immediate physical reaction in people who have social anxiety, which can be very upsetting and difficult to regulate. This contributes to the overall unpleasantness of the symptoms. The following are a few bodily signs of acute social anxiety (Mayo Clinic, 2017):

increased heart rate

shaky or shaking; blushing; dry lips; dizziness or fear of fainting; difficult and stuttering speech; muscle soreness and tension, generally in the upper body; slower brain processes or an inability to focus or concentrate; sweating of the palms; chest tightness or a choking sensation;

These physical symptoms are comparable to those that occur during a panic attack (although social anxiety and panic attacks are two very different conditions) or after being in an accident or being in a situation where you believe that you could be physically harmed. Notably, these responses happen in social situations where there isn't a serious risk of physical harm to you. However, they resemble responses you would have when you're being threatened with harm. Most people consider these social situations pleasant or harmless even though they cause you to experience such terrifying bodily sensations. Reactions to severe social anxiety are powerful, overwhelming, and out of proportion to any possible danger.

Section Four

Awareness and Mindfulness: In order to reduce stress and calm the body and mind, mindfulness practices include breathing exercises, guided imagery, and other methods.

There Are Numerous Benefits to Mindfulness - Uncover the Completeness of the Here and Now

Apart from the well-tried method of meditation, there are a few extremely easy ways to increase our awareness of day-to-day activities. Because of our cushion or chair training, we can use almost any situation to identify and track feelings, experiences, and thoughts as they arise without needless effort or judgment. Here are five strategies for becoming more aware of the present moment. The Buddha would be happy.

1. Just take a breath

Often, the focus of meditation is just on paying attention to your breath. You can maintain mindfulness outside the cushion by focusing on the sensation of breath coming into and out of your nose or feeling your stomach rise and fall.

Though you always breathe, how often do you notice it? Increase the duration of your sitting exercises by learning to pay attention to your breathing at work, school, or traveling. Pay attention to your breathing, whether waiting for the bus, in line at the grocery store, in traffic, or just before or after a meal. Taking one deliberate breath provides instantaneous awareness of the present moment and could be the most straightforward method of developing mindfulness.

2. Go for a stroll

Step outside and walk mindfully and with purpose.

Choose a nice area to walk and spend a few minutes focusing on each step. Pay attention to the pressure they feel as your feet hit the ground and lift back up. Observe how your legs and toes cooperate to propel your body forward.

If you can, incorporate walking meditation into your practice regularly.

3. Develop an Appreciation for Quiet

Being quiet is a good condition for mindfulness. Acknowledge it and investigate it.

Our lives are not at all peaceful. The music or show we turn on fills the void left by the absence of distractions like traffic, planes passing overhead, coworkers or fellow students chatting away, or the ping of a phone call or message.

Find silence and spend some time in it. You'll find sounds like wind, rustling leaves, birdsong, animals, rain, and so forth that can be heard even in the most isolated places. Make advantage of the sounds that arise from the silence as part of your mindfulness exercise. Examine any tension you may get when you don't employ your usual diversions, then release them so you can resume the exquisite practice of focused listening.

4. Give Up Being Busy

Concentrating on one thing at a time is one of the easiest and toughest methods to improve mindfulness.

Consider what happens if you take a brief break from multitasking. To ensure every work or project has your attention, finish one before moving on to the next. Turn off your smartphone, disable any mind-numbing apps, and reduce background noise to eliminate as many distractions as possible. Now, focus on one item at a time, whether you're writing an important speech, painting furniture, or eating breakfast.

As you would when meditating, softly but forcefully bring them back and keep your entire attention on the task at hand.

5. Tasks Are Important

Cooking, cleaning, eating, folding laundry, and tooth brushing are still necessary. Make good use of your time.

While you do your business, give your all to the tasks around the house. You'll feel much more grateful in addition to having a more organized garage, spotless windows, and a cleaner bathroom.

Pay close attention to what you eat when you are eating—not just the food that ends up on your fork, but also the ingredients that were used to prepare the meal in the first place. Feeding you entails an incredible network of interdependencies, ranging from the workers who tilled the soil to the beekeepers who made the tires that carried your food to you and all the way around. You'll discover countless reasons to be grateful once you consider it.

7. Acquire proper breathing techniques: Doesn't it sound absurd? But most of us don't use our breath to its full potential. Intense, slow breathing has many calming effects. When you are worried or upset, concentrate on your breathing for a few minutes. You'll quickly discover that using your breath can help you cultivate inner peace.

How do you breathe efficiently? Inhale, hold, release, hold. Proceed at your own pace. This might be your pause button when it seems like the world is moving too fast.

8. Get in touch with nature

The mental state of nature is relaxing. Engage with nature for a while to cultivate inner peace. Don't be afraid to take risks; you can be conservative and still be successful.

How can I spend more time in nature? Go for a stroll in the park, work in your garden, or just sit and see the clouds drift by. Yosemite National Park and Sea of Thieves:

9. Express gratitude

If you are grateful, you may be able to concentrate more on what you currently have than what you lack. It's a fast route to inner serenity. Develop the routine of listing your blessings in your gratitude journal. Focusing on the good things that happened during the day could change how we view it.

How do you show your appreciation? List three things that you were happy about today. They could be as simple as a satisfying supper or a good laugh.

10. Pay attention to acceptance:

There are many unknown and uncontrollable factors in life. Instead of wishing things were different, try embracing them as they are. That is embracing reality and working with it rather than against it, not giving up or being passive.

How may my acceptance be strengthened? Try not to criticize your feelings as they arise or subside when life throws you a curveball. Sometimes, we can overcome a situation's power over us by accepting it.

11. Practice non-judgment: It's critical to develop the ability to analyze your ideas and emotions without assigning them a positive or negative label. By practicing non-judgment, you create room for acceptance and inner peace.

What kind of nonjudgment do you practice? Remember that it's just a thought when you catch yourself passing judgment. It'll be gone as quickly as a cloud in the sky.

12. Promote closer ties:

Form relationships that uplift your soul. Spend time with those that uplift and make you happy. While you shouldn't steer clear of all challenging relationships, you should try to surround yourself with a strong support system of kind and considerate individuals.

How can our ties get stronger? Spend time with loved ones or contact a friend who can help you feel heard and supported. Engage in those conversations. These times spent together can unexpectedly help us feel at ease.

Recall that there aren't universally applicable answers here. Choose what resonates with you, try different things, and find your path to inner peace. We are available to help you. We're here for you every step of the way, offering everything from breathing exercises to help you harness the power of your breath to guided meditations to help you build calmness and peaceful soundscapes to take you there.

Unwind mentally. Change the world in some way.

The Nervous System: An Essential Organ!

Nearly every function in your body is managed by your nervous system, from causing your mouth to moisten just before you eat your favorite dish to quickly removing your hand from a scorching cooktop when you unintentionally lean on it.

Your nervous system is divided into two main sections: the voluntary and involuntary components.

The voluntary nervous system is responsible for all of your conscious movements. Your voluntary nervous system comes into action when you go for your phone to check how flawless everyone else's life appears on social media.

On the other hand, you receive no direct information from the involuntary nervous system, often known as the autonomic nervous system. This portion of the nervous system is responsible for your digestion. You don't have to pay attention to your stomach when you eat because it releases precisely one cup of stomach acid and enzymes to help digest that hamburger you just finished. That all happens automatically, behind the scenes. Just think of how much more we would have to accomplish!

Other examples of the involuntary portion include your heart rate, pupil dilation, and temperature management (sweating or experiencing goosebumps). They are not directly under our control. However, your nervous system does! Your heart rate increases when you're upset because your nervous system requires it. Because of all those butterflies taking up room in your stomach when you're deeply in love, your digestive system acts differently (that's your nervous system again). Your nervous system receives signals from your amygdala when it believes you are in danger. It then initiates the whole fight-or-flight reaction.

The involuntary portion of the nervous system is where our emotions impact our organs.

The problem lies in the fact that prolonged abuse will cause your nervous system to become so worn out and weary that it will significantly increase in sensitivity. Even though the trigger was something that wouldn't scare other people—not even the "old you" of a few months ago—it will take less and less to bring it on full force and deliver all of the effects of a bout of anxiety.

Here's a brief explanation of this procedure. Imagine yourself in the water, swimming and warding off two ravenous sharks. You swim like a dolphin, so they can't bite you, but they get very close, and you have to shout them offensive names for them to turn around. You're feeling very worn out from having to battle for your life this time, and your nervous system is still tense from the confrontation.

While swimming towards the coast, you spot the fin of a tiny, graceful, and completely safe baby whale in your proximity. Something magical that would have otherwise brought you joy. But because your nervous system has grown extremely sensitive, you now experience intense anxiety. You were just scared by something good.

Your nervous system will become more sensitive with more anxiety or panic episodes you have. You can then become extremely apprehensive about something that shouldn't even cause you to feel nervous.

For this reason, you may notice that it takes less and less for you to get frightened over time. For this very reason, one of the main causes of worry is the nervous system. In part two, we'll focus on soothing and letting it heal. Are you prepared to do it?

Everybody handles stress differently. Everyone has gone through horrific experiences, and after a few months, the agony and memory of the events begin to fade. We're going to be ready to handle life in this way. Could you picture yourself experiencing the same level of intensity and sincerity of grief five years after losing a loved one? That is not a life we could lead. However, PTSD patients cannot stop thinking about their horrific previous experiences. Over time, this causes a significant disruption in the sufferer's life.

The core causes of all six anxiety disorders are pathological anxiety and atypical brain chemistry. The majority of people will suffer from one of these ailments. However, some people may show symptoms of multiple illnesses, their behavior may change over time, or one condition may progress to another. It's important to identify and understand the type of anxiety you may have, but it's also critical to realize how each condition functions and how it affects other disorders. As usual, go see your doctor!

Chapter 8: The Ability to Shift

advantages of change

It can be challenging to embrace change and adjust to new circumstances, but it is an inherent aspect of life. Success and personal development depend on our ability to accept change, whether from changes in our personal or professional lives. The five phases of embracing change and how to go through them will be discussed in this article.

First stage: denial

Denial is the first step before accepting change. This is what happens when we don't acknowledge that something is changing or that it will have an impact on us. Feelings of panic, anxiety, or shock could cause us to want to ignore or completely avoid the change. Feeling denial when faced with change is normal, yet this might impede development.

It's critical to acknowledge and embrace that change is occurring in order to get over denial. Give the shift some thought and reflection, and ask friends, family, or a therapist for help if needed.

Phase Two: Opposition

Resistance is the second stage of accepting change. We aggressively oppose change during this period and may experience resentment, frustration, or anger. We can believe the change is unjust or will negatively affect us.

Finding the sources of your resistance is essential to overcoming it. Do you have a fear of the unknown? Do you fear losing anything significant to you? After determining where it originated, you can begin creating a strategy to overcome your resistance.

Phase Three: Investigation

Exploration is the third stage of accepting change. At this point, we start looking into the opportunities and possibilities that change might present. In the future, we could experience curiosity, excitement, or hope.

It's critical to maintain an open mind and a curiosity about change in order to welcome discovery. Seek new experiences and opportunities that may present themselves, as well as methods to grow and learn from change.

Phase Four: Acknowledgment

Acceptance is the fourth stage of embracing change. At this point, we embrace change and start adjusting to our new situation. We might start to appreciate the positive features of the transition and feel more at ease with it.

It's critical to keep your attention on the here and now and the potential benefits of change to embrace acceptance. Seek to maximize your new circumstances and cultivate gratitude for everything that you have in your life.

Step 5: Consolidation

Integration is the last stage of embracing change. At this point, we accept change as a part of our path and fully integrate it into our lives. Change may provide us with a sense of increased self-assurance, adaptability, and resilience.

In order to welcome integration, one must always adapt to and learn from change. Seek fresh chances for both professional and personal development, as well as methods to use your newly acquired knowledge and abilities.

To sum up, acceptance of change goes through five stages: denial, acceptance, exploration, resistance, and integration. You may face change with courage, resilience, and flexibility if you can acknowledge and accept it, pinpoint the causes of your resistance, investigate the opportunities and possibilities that change may bring, embrace acceptance, and integrate change into your life. Recall that change is a necessary component of life and that success and personal development depend on your ability to accept and adjust to it.

Without realizing it, change is something we frequently oppose.

Whether you choose to welcome it or not, it will still enter your life. It is quite simple to adjust when making the change since it is something you want.

However, are unforeseen and unplanned changes harmful? What if every modification was accepted by default?

In general, when I reflect on my life, I see that everything positive that has happened to me is a direct outcome of past adjustments.

While most individuals stay in their comfort zones, I think making the first move toward change can significantly impact your life.

A few advantages of the modification are listed below:

Individual development

You always have the chance to develop and pick up new skills when something changes. Gain fresh perspectives on various facets of your existence. Lessons that did not lead to your desired outcome can also be learned via adjustments.

Adaptability

You can more readily adjust to new circumstances, surroundings, and people if you undergo frequent changes. In this manner, you avoid being angry when something unexpected happens.

Enhancements

Everyone wishes they could have better relationships, homes, careers, finances, and other aspects of their lives. It is a well-known fact that nothing improves by itself. In order to do this, we must alter how we do things. There could be no improvements without change.

Life Principles

Occasionally, life events force you to reassess your situation and view things from a fresh angle. Your life values might also be strengthened, depending on the shift.

The domino effects

We frequently give up when we cannot finish implementing a significant, instant change. That's when seemingly insignificant adjustments start to add up. Small steps taken one at a time will eventually bring about the desired large improvement.

Power

Life's challenging periods can occasionally result from transitions. Unfortunately, life is not a fairy tale, and we have to deal with bad things happening to us. Surviving a challenging time will strengthen you.

Advancement

Changes spark progress. They enable progress and development in the situation.

Prospects

You can never be sure what a change will bring. Diverging from your typical route will present you with a plethora of alternatives. New options for contentment and happiness will result from the adjustments.

fresh starts

Every alteration signifies a new chapter. It's time to conclude this chapter and open a new one. Changes provide excitement and fresh beginnings.

Customs

A life that is utterly dull, very predictable, and uninteresting. If nothing changed, your life would be like this.

Therefore, the next time you find yourself tempted to fight or avoid change, try to start the changes that will move you toward your goals.

www.ingramcontent.com/pod-product-compliance
Lightning Source LLC
Chambersburg PA
CBHW052141110526
44591CB00012B/1806